VERMONT

A Summer View

Ramon Scavelli

To Bill,
my good friend of
many years. With good
wishes and appreciation

Ramon Scavelli
1995

The New England Press
Shelburne, Vermont

To Wynne and Bob Benson, for giving us the key.

ISBN 1-881535-10-X
Library of Congress Catalog Card Number: 94-65733

For additional copies or for a catalog of our other titles, please write:

The New England Press
P.O. Box 575
Shelburne, VT 05482

Printed in Hong Kong
through Four Colour Imports, Ltd.
Louisville, Kentucky

Acknowledgments

I would like to thank Al and Maggie Rosa of the New England Press for the opportunity. A special thanks goes to editor Mark Wanner, for his commitment, vision, enthusiasm, and guidance in making this effort a reality.

I would also like to thank Joseph Fisher of Malaga, New Jersey, who for fifty years has been my constant friend and mentor.

Finally, I thank my wife, Joan, for sharing with me the Vermont Experience.

Ramon Scavelli
March 1994

A Summer View

Each summer for the past decade, my wife Joan and I have traveled north to experience Vermont. When viewing Vermont perfection, whatever that may be, I can't help but remember the words of James Russell Lowell, "And what is so rare as a day in June? Then if ever perfect days, then heaven tries the earth if it be in tune and over it softly her warm ears lay." With these few words, Lowell says it all.

From our summer place, as we like to call it, in Jeffersonville, Vermont, we have traveled the state with enthusiasm, and a desire to be a part of it, if only for four or five weeks. We have our favorite towns, churches, covered bridges, antique barns, country stores, county fairs, and scenic views. We revisit them year after year. But the surprise of discovery is ever present in our quest for the photograph and the enjoyment of nature.

I am a person who is happily able to pursue careers in more than one area—as a violist in the National Symphony Orchestra of Washington, D.C. and as a photographer. My love affair with photography has led to numerous one-man shows and national and international recognition from books, magazines, record covers, and television. For the most part, the double life in the arts has worked well for me.

After an intense year-long effort in the performing arts, summer means vacation, Vermont, and total devotion to the visual arts. Vermont offers the challenge to present not only the scenic view, but to present everything—the architecture, activities, colors—that we love most in the state.

Why is Vermont so special to us? Is it because its summer green is greener than any place we know? Is it the clear days and cool nights? Or is it the people? Whether natives or flatlanders, Vermonters have a special pride and interest in their land, their environment, their villages. Thus Vermont retains its beautiful, clean air and well-cared-for communities. Their pride and devotion to the land is contagious. Seeing the land violated in our own suburban community, we come to our special place each summer, treading softly with respect and a quiet love for all that is around us.

We relish the evening visits of deer, and the goshawk that lives in the old elm tree. We remember the startling midnight visit of a mother and baby raccoon that sounded like the bear that was seen in the area—and, of course, we remember our first sighting of the bear itself.

The contrast of our lives between Washington, D.C. and Vermont is striking. The hectic world of the performing arts contrasts with the relaxation of watching a quiet but active beaver pond beside a country road. The fast lane of the clogged Beltway compares with a country lane leading into the hills. The sounds of traffic and construction contrast with the music of rippling mountain streams after a summer rain, some flowing under covered bridges that add tranquility and a serene beauty to the scene.

Our summer activities take us even farther away from the pressures of the city. The rainy afternoons spent antiquing, always with the anticipation of discovery. The country store—with its polished marble counter, old-fashioned soda fountain, ice cream sodas, and penny candy—that survives as an ornament of stability in the community and evokes the feeling of summers past. The county fair with its bright-eyed children, sparkling clean animals, and assorted smells. The swimming hole and excursions downriver on an innertube or in a canoe. The Sunday afternoon ball game behind the schoolhouse, or the band concert on the green where you can get to know your neighbors.

Photographing this portrait of summer has been a rewarding experience. Hopefully the photographs presented in the following pages will entice, encourage, and maybe inspire you to travel in search of your own special corner of Vermont.

Next to our favorite covered bridge, north of Waterville, I can contemplate the flurry of activities of the past year and the Vermont summer now drawing to a close. In this beautiful setting, with the soothing flow of the North Branch of the Lamoille River passing by, the burn-out and fatigue are gone. As we return to city life, it is with a spirit of renewal and purpose for the musical months that lie ahead.

Flower Barn

Jeffersonville

Barton (*opposite*

Summer Harvest

Fresh Produce for Sale

Long gone are the days when cows outnumbered people, but cows, horses, oxen, and other animals still play important roles in Vermont's rural life. After enduring the cold, white winter months, they are rewarded with acres and acres of lush greenery. Whether working hard to pull a load, making new friends, or "hanging out" in the barnyard, the animals, like us, make the most of the precious months of summer in Vermont.

Mount Mansfield from Cambridge

Moss Glen Falls *(opposite)*

Country Stroll

Vermont 1939

Black-Eyed Susans, South Walden

Fishing the Lamoille

Reading

Woodland Cathedral *(opposite)*

Vermont's clear air and beautiful countryside beckon everyone to get out and explore. Climbing a wooded trail up and up to a panoramic view from a windswept summit; following country roads that sometimes seem to lead nowhere at all; jumping into a swimming hole, the plunge and the cold, clear water equally breathtaking—these are just a few of the ways to enjoy an active Vermont summer.

First Congregational Church, Bennington

Dog Days of Summer (Jesse)

Vermont Billboard

Smugglers Notch *(opposite*

Waiting for Winter

Barnscape

Helping Hand

North of Burke Hollow

With all of the glorious views around Vermont, it can be easy to forget about the little things that add to summer's splendor. A single flower or leaf can capture the vibrance of a midsummer day, or the hint of autumn that comes with a cool August rain. A dewy spider web reminds one of the warm, still summer morning. A close look will reveal the many, many small scenes that add up to summertime in Vermont.

Summer Treat

Bennington Monument *(opposite)*

Gone Swimming

Summer Color

Refreshing Pause, Battery Park

A Look Back *(opposite)*

Kilgore's Country Store

Strafford Meeting House

A freshly cut hayfield is one of the treasures of summer. The fresh smell of the grass can clear the mind, even as it tickles the nose. The rows of cut hay or the neatly arranged rolls or bales can turn a sunny vista into a tapestry, a work of art. For the farmers, it is a time of hard work and hope—it is not beauty they pursue, but dry hay under cover. For the rest of us, it is a time to savor the bounty of the land in Vermont summertime.

Valley Pride and Paula

Round Church, Richmond

Flowers and Sky

Out to Pasture

Newfane

Cambridge

Still Life

United Church of Craftsbury *(opposite)*

Rockingham Meeting House

East Hardwick

Light and Color